PRAYERSCRIPTS

DISCERN THE ENEMY

30 *Days of Prayers for*

SHARPENING SPIRITUAL PERCEPTION TO RECOGNIZE SATAN'S TACTICS AND GUARD YOUR DESTINY

CYRIL OPOKU

Discern the Enemy: Sharpening Spiritual Perception to Recognize Satan's Tactics and Guard Your Destiny

© 2025 Cyril Opoku. *PrayerScripts*. All rights reserved.

Published by *Quest Publications*

ISBN: 978-1-988439-76-1

Cover design by *Quest Publications (questpublications@outlook.com)*

Unless otherwise indicated, all Scripture quotations are taken from the World English Bible WEB, which is in the public domain. For more information, visit: www.worldenglish.bible

This book is a work of devotional encouragement. It is not intended to replace biblical study, pastoral counsel, or professional therapy.

Printed in the United States of America.

First Edition: August 2025

For more books like this, visit *PrayerScripts:* https://prayerscripts.org

CONTENTS

PREFACE

"But solid food is for those who are full grown, who by reason of use have their senses exercised to discern good and evil."
—Hebrews 5:14 WEB

Discernment is one of the most vital weapons of the believer. In a world filled with deception, distraction, and disguised wickedness, God calls His people to sharpen their spiritual perception and distinguish between what is of Him and what is of the enemy. Discernment is not mere intuition; it is the Spirit-enabled ability to see beyond appearances, to expose hidden agendas, and to guard our lives and families from the subtle snares of Satan.

This book, *Discern the Enemy*, has been written as part of the *Exposing the Enemy* series to equip you with Scripture-based prayers that will sharpen your vision, heighten your awareness, and anchor your spirit in truth. Each prayer flows directly from the Word of God, turning biblical insight into prophetic declarations of power.

As you walk through these pages, expect God to awaken your senses. Expect hidden tactics to be revealed. Expect clarity to replace confusion. And above all, expect to grow in the kind of spiritual sharpness that protects your destiny and aligns your steps with the will of God.

At His command,
Cyril O. *(Illinois, August 2025)*

INTRODUCTION

The greatest danger is not the enemy you can see—it is the one you cannot. Satan rarely attacks in obvious ways. Instead, he works through whispers, disguises, and carefully crafted distractions. Many destinies have been derailed not because the enemy was stronger, but because he remained undetected.

That is why discernment is essential for every believer who desires to walk in victory. To discern is to pierce through the fog of deception and recognize what lies beneath. It is to see the serpent hiding in the grass before it strikes. It is to sense the counterfeit before it entangles you. Without discernment, the believer is vulnerable. With discernment, the believer is unshakable.

This book is not written to stir fear, but to ignite confidence. The Spirit of God has promised to give you wisdom, knowledge, and perception that go beyond human reasoning. As you journey through *Discern the Enemy*, you will discover how to anchor yourself in the Word of God so deeply that the enemy's schemes cannot deceive you. Every prayer is designed to train your spirit, sharpen your mind, and strengthen your heart to walk as a watchman over your life and family.

As you open these pages, come with expectation. This is more than a book; it is a training ground for your spirit. Each Scripture and prayer is a weapon forged to cut through deception and expose the hidden works of darkness. If you will engage with faith, persistence, and the guidance of the Holy Spirit, you will not only recognize the enemy's tactics—you will rise above them, walking in wisdom, clarity, and unshakable victory.

How to Use This Book

This is not a book to be rushed through. Each of the 30 prayers is structured as a daily prayer journey, combining the Word of God with prophetic, Spirit-led intercession. Here's how you can make the most of it:

1. **Start with the Scripture** – Each prayer begins with a verse from the World English Bible (WEB). Read it slowly and aloud, letting the Word sink into your heart.

2. **Declare the Word** – Meditate on the key truth in the verse, affirming it as God's unchanging promise.

3. **Pray with Authority** – Use the written prayer as a guide. Speak it boldly, personally, and with conviction. Replace "I" with your name or the names of loved ones as needed.

4. **Journal Insights** – Keep a notebook nearby. Write down any impressions, warnings, or directions you sense from the Holy Spirit. Discernment grows when you act on what God reveals.

5. **Build a Rhythm** – Pray one Scripture each day, or linger longer on those that strike you deeply. Repetition builds sharpness, and sharpness builds victory.

Whether you walk through these prayers privately in your devotional time, with your family, or in a small group, the key is consistency. Each prayer is a sword in your hand—use it faithfully.

DAY 1

The Mind of Christ Revealed

"For who has known the mind of the Lord, that he should instruct him? But we have Christ's mind."
— 1 Corinthians 2:16 WEB

Mighty God, I rise today declaring that I carry the mind of Christ, and by Your Spirit I will not walk in confusion, blindness, or deception. Every scheme of the adversary is exposed before me because the light of Christ shines in my heart and sharpens my discernment. I declare that I will not be tricked, manipulated, or misled, for You have given me eyes to see, ears to hear, and a heart to understand.

Lord, I call upon the Spirit of wisdom and revelation to illuminate the paths of my life. Let every counterfeit voice be silenced. Let every shadow of deception be chased away. I ask that You train my spirit to recognize the hidden snares, the subtle temptations, and the traps of distraction that the enemy lays before me. Father, sharpen my discernment so that no plan of the wicked one can advance unnoticed in my home, my family, or my future.

I stand as a watchman over my household, refusing to allow the enemy to creep in through deceit or disguise. Let the light of truth expose every dark scheme. Let the Spirit of Christ in me separate what is holy from what is corrupt, what is eternal from what is temporary, and what is of heaven from what is of hell.

Today I proclaim that I will walk in the clarity of Christ's mind. My decisions are Spirit-led, my steps are sure, and my discernment is sharp. Every enemy is unmasked, every lie is uncovered, and every scheme is revealed by the wisdom of my God. In Jesus' name, Amen.

DAY 2

Sharpened by the Spirit

But solid food is for those who are full grown, who by reason of use have their senses exercised to discern good and evil.
— Hebrews 5:14 WEB

Mighty God of light and truth, I rise today declaring that my eyes shall not be dimmed by deception, nor my ears dulled by lies. You have called me into maturity in Christ, to walk in spiritual sharpness and holy perception. Lord, I refuse to live blind to the snares of the enemy. I will not stumble in ignorance or be tricked by the schemes of darkness, for You have given me the Spirit of wisdom and understanding.

Father, train my inner senses by the power of Your Word. Just as muscles grow by exercise, let my discernment grow through constant use. Open my eyes to recognize evil in its subtle disguises. Strip away every veil that hides wickedness, whether it comes cloaked in flattering speech, enticing opportunities, or counterfeit light. By Your Spirit, let me see beyond appearances into the true nature of things.

Lord, expose the enemy's strategies against me, my household, and every area of my destiny. Grant me clarity to discern the difference between what comes from You and what is sown by the adversary. Let no whisper of deception penetrate my spirit. Teach me to test all things and hold fast to what is good.

I declare that my family shall walk in divine awareness. We will not fall prey to false counsel, hidden traps, or satanic agendas. Our senses are sharpened, and our discernment is exercised. We will stand in the light of truth and move with accuracy in Your will.

In Jesus' name, Amen.

DAY 3

TEST THE SPIRITS

"Beloved, don't believe every spirit, but test the spirits, whether they are of God, because many false prophets have gone out into the world."
—1 John 4:1 WEB

Mighty Father, God of light and truth, I rise today with boldness, declaring that I will not be deceived by the lies of the enemy. You have called me and my family to walk in truth, and I will not allow the spirit of error or deception to have any influence over our lives. Lord, sharpen my discernment so that I may expose every counterfeit spirit that seeks to infiltrate my home, my relationships, and my walk with You.

I declare that every mask of falsehood will be torn away. Let every hidden agenda of darkness be revealed before me, and let me see with the eyes of Your Spirit. Lord, grant me the ability to distinguish truth from error, the holy from the profane, and righteousness from the counterfeit righteousness that the enemy parades before me.

I reject the whispers of seduction and manipulation that try to ensnare my mind. Holy Spirit, saturate me with wisdom and alertness, that I may identify and dismantle every lie planted by the enemy. I decree that no spirit of confusion or deception will find a foothold in my household.

Father, make me a watchman over my family, exposing spiritual threats before they strike. Cause me to discern the subtle schemes of the adversary, that every trap may be avoided and every snare broken. By Your Spirit, I will walk in clarity, purity, and truth.

In Jesus' name, Amen.

DAY 4

LED INTO ALL TRUTH

However when he, the Spirit of truth, has come, he will guide you into all truth. For he will not speak from himself; but whatever he hears, he will speak. He will declare to you things that are coming.
— John 16:13 WEB

Mighty Spirit of Truth, I lift my heart before You with a cry for divine discernment. You are the One who guides me into all truth, exposing every lie of the enemy. Today, I declare that my spirit is aligned with Yours, and my ears are tuned to the whisper of heaven. I will not stumble in darkness, nor will my family be deceived, because Your light unveils every hidden snare.

Lord, sharpen my perception so that I may discern between the schemes of Satan and the will of God. Let no false voice, no counterfeit spirit, and no deceitful doctrine take root in my home. Strip the disguise from every agent of the enemy, whether they come as wolves in sheep's clothing or serpents in the grass. Grant me the wisdom to see beyond the surface and the courage to stand firm in truth.

Spirit of the Living God, declare to me what is to come, that I may be prepared and not caught off guard. As You reveal, I will walk boldly in faith, covering my family with the shield of truth. Every hidden trap is exposed, every subtle whisper of the enemy is silenced, and every scheme is brought to light under the authority of Christ.

Thank You, Lord, for making my eyes sharp, my heart steady, and my path secure. My family will not walk blind, for Your Spirit is our guide. The light of truth prevails over every shadow of deception.

In Jesus' name, Amen.

DAY 5

WISE AS SERPENTS

"Behold, I send you out as sheep among wolves. Therefore
be wise as serpents and harmless as doves."
— Matthew 10:16 WEB

Mighty Father, the All-Knowing God, I stand in awe of Your
wisdom that surpasses all understanding. You have sent me into
this world as a sheep among wolves, but You have not left me
defenseless. By the power of Your Spirit, I embrace the call to walk
with discernment and holy perception. Lord, sharpen my spiritual
senses so that I may not fall prey to deception, distraction, or
disguise of the enemy.

I declare that I will not be naïve to the schemes of darkness. I will
discern between truth and error, light and shadow, righteousness
and wickedness. By Your Spirit, I will detect the wolf that wears
sheep's clothing and expose every hidden snare set before my
household. No subtle whisper of the adversary will go unnoticed,
for my ears are tuned to the Shepherd's voice and the voice of a
stranger I will not follow.

Grant me wisdom to tread carefully, strategically, and victoriously.
Let me be as harmless as a dove, walking in purity and peace, yet as
sharp and discerning as a serpent, unmasking the craftiness of evil.
May my family be covered under this grace of wisdom, never
entangled by the lies of Satan.

Today I receive the mantle of discernment afresh. I decree that confusion will not cloud my judgment, nor will fear blind my eyes. The Spirit of Truth empowers me to see clearly, to hear rightly, and to move with holy accuracy. Wolves will be exposed, traps revealed, and strategies of hell overturned.

In Jesus' name, Amen.

DAY 6

DIVINE LIGHT REVEALS PATHS

Your word is a lamp to my feet, and a light to my path.
— Psalm 119:105 WEB

O Sovereign Lord, I come before You as a warrior armed with Your truth, declaring that Your Word is my eternal lamp and guiding light. I refuse to walk in darkness or be deceived by the enemy's cunning schemes. Illuminate every hidden snare, every subtle trap laid to divert me or my household from Your purposes. Let Your light pierce every shadow that seeks to obscure Your divine direction.

Father, I ask You to sharpen my spiritual sight, that I may discern the whispers of the adversary from Your voice. As I navigate my daily steps, reveal to me the spiritual patterns and tactics that the enemy deploys to disrupt my family, my work, and my destiny. Empower me to recognize deception in every form, that I may stand firm, unshaken, and guided by Your truth.

Let every counsel of darkness be exposed and rendered powerless in the light of Your Word. I decree clarity and insight over every situation, proclaiming that no scheme of the enemy can operate in secrecy under the authority of Christ in my life. Lead me by Your lamp, O Lord, into paths of righteousness, safety, and divine favor.

I receive the wisdom to discern, the courage to act, and the grace to walk boldly in Your light. Let the enemy's plans crumble at the brilliance of Your Word, and let my family dwell securely in Your protection. I claim the light of God's truth over every shadow of deception, and I will not be moved.

In Jesus' name, Amen.

DAY 7

WISDOM TO DISCERN TACTICS

But if any of you lacks wisdom, let him ask of God, who
gives to all liberally and without reproach, and it shall be
given to him.
— James 1:5 WEB

Almighty Father, I call upon Your infinite wisdom today, declaring
that You are my source of understanding and spiritual insight. I
refuse to be ignorant of the enemy's devices. Lord, grant me
supernatural wisdom to identify the lies, manipulations, and
schemes designed to derail my life and the lives of my loved ones.
Open my eyes to the hidden tactics that seek to weaken my faith
and disrupt my family's peace.

Heavenly Father, I pray for the discernment that separates truth
from deception, light from darkness. Let Your Spirit illuminate
every corner of my mind, exposing hidden snares and cunning
strategies of the adversary. As I walk daily, let Your wisdom be my
compass, directing my decisions and strengthening my spiritual
perception. Equip me to respond with authority and faith, not fear,
against every plot formed in secret.

Lord, I decree that every hidden plan of the enemy is unmasked
before Your throne. Let no lie or manipulation succeed against me
or my household. Instill in me the ability to anticipate attacks,
discern intentions, and navigate every challenge with the mind of

Christ. May my choices and steps reflect Your divine guidance and wisdom at all times.

I claim Your promise that wisdom flows freely to me as I seek You earnestly. I stand firm, confident that Your Spirit will guide me into full awareness of the enemy's tactics and deliver my family into divine protection. I will walk boldly, shielded and enlightened, in Your all-encompassing wisdom.

In Jesus' name, Amen.

DAY 8

Trust Guides Every Step

Trust in the LORD with all your heart, and lean not on
your own understanding; in all your ways acknowledge
him, and he will direct your paths.
— Proverbs 3:5-6 WEB

Lord Almighty, I lift my heart to You, declaring that my trust rests
fully in You, not in my own insight or human understanding. I ask
that You expose every deception, every hidden snare set by the
enemy to confuse, mislead, or harm me and my family. Let Your
Spirit guide me with clarity and discernment in every step I take.

Father, teach me to rely on Your direction above all else. Remove
every trace of doubt, distraction, and manipulation that seeks to
divert me from Your perfect path. Open my spiritual eyes to
recognize the enemy's tactics and grant me the courage to act
decisively, armed with Your wisdom and strength. May my heart
remain unwavering in trust, even when challenges seem
overwhelming.

I decree that no plan of darkness can succeed against my household.
Every scheme intended to disrupt our peace, health, or prosperity
is nullified and rendered powerless. I acknowledge You in all my
ways, and I receive Your guidance to walk securely and victoriously.
Your wisdom will illuminate every decision, every relationship, and
every circumstance.

Lord, I walk confidently, knowing that my trust in You exposes the enemy's lies and brings Your perfect order into my life. May every step I take be guided by Your divine insight, ensuring safety, protection, and victory for me and my loved ones.

In Jesus' name, Amen.

DAY 9

TEST EVERYTHING IN LIGHT

Prove what is pleasing to the Lord.
— Ephesians 5:10 WEB

Mighty God, I come boldly before Your throne, declaring my commitment to discern what is truly pleasing in Your sight. I refuse to be misled by the enemy's deceptive tactics. Reveal every scheme and hidden agenda that seeks to corrupt my heart, misdirect my thoughts, or disrupt my household. Let Your Spirit grant me supernatural perception to test all circumstances and uncover every plan of darkness.

Lord, sharpen my ability to differentiate between what aligns with Your will and what originates from the enemy. May my heart, mind, and spirit be sensitive to Your guidance, and may I not be persuaded by appearances, flattery, or falsehoods. Grant me the discernment to expose the enemy's manipulations and the wisdom to act in accordance with Your Word.

I decree that all evil schemes are revealed and rendered powerless. Let every plan that contradicts Your will be dismantled and consumed by Your light. Protect my family and me from deception, and let our steps be firmly established in righteousness, truth, and Your divine approval.

Father, I commit to testing everything, seeking Your approval in all things, and exposing the enemy at every turn. Empower me with spiritual insight that transforms uncertainty into clarity and fear into confident obedience. May my life reflect Your light and truth as I navigate every attack with discernment.

In Jesus' name, Amen.

DAY 10

EXPOSE AND REJECT DECEPTION

But test all things; hold fast what is good.
— 1 Thessalonians 5:21 WEB

Heavenly Father, I approach Your throne declaring that I will test every thought, every message, and every influence according to Your truth. I refuse to be ensnared by the enemy's lies or the subtle manipulations that seek to harm me and my loved ones. Grant me supernatural discernment to detect every hidden attack and to reject what is not from You.

Lord, empower me to hold fast to what is good, embracing Your wisdom, guidance, and promises in every circumstance. Let every deception be unmasked, every lie exposed, and every plan of darkness nullified. Protect my family and me from spiritual confusion, emotional manipulation, and every form of hidden sabotage. May our hearts be anchored in Your Word, discerning and steadfast.

I declare that I will not be led astray by appearances, persuasion, or cunning strategies. Every scheme of the enemy will be revealed and rendered powerless under the authority of Christ. Strengthen my spiritual insight, Father, so that I may respond with boldness and faith, standing as a light in every situation.

Lord, let my life be a testimony of discernment and divine protection. May my family and I walk in clarity, embracing only what is good and pleasing to You, exposing the enemy at every turn.